HANNIBAL

HANNIBAL

BY
ROBERT GREEN

A FIRST BOOK

FRANKLIN WATTS
A DIVISION OF GROLIER PUBLISHING
NEW YORK – LONDON – HONG KONG – SYDNEY
DANBURY, CONNECTICUT

For D.R. Green

Cover design by Robin Hoffmann

Map by MacArt Design

Photo credits ©: Art Resource: cover, pp. 2 (both photos Alinari), 16, 42 (both photos Scala); Bettmann Archive: pp. 25, 26, 39, 53; Bridgeman Art Library: pp 45, 48, 49, 50; Mary Evans Picture Library: pp. 21, 32; North Wind Picture Archives: pp. 19, 23, 35, 37; Stock Montage, Inc.: pp. 8, 11, 14, 55, 57; UPI/Bettmann: p. 13.

Consultant: Allen M. Ward, University of Connecticut.

Library of Congress Cataloging-in-Publication Data

Green, Robert.
Hannibal / by Robert Green.
p.   cm. — (A First Book)
Includes bibliographical references and index.
Summary: Presents the life and military exploits of the famous
Carthaginian general.
ISBN 0-531-20240-2 (lib. bdg.) — ISBN 0-531-15811-X (pbk.)
1. Hannibal, 247–182 B.C.—Juvenile literature.   2. Generals—Tunisia—
Carthage (Extinct city)—Biography—Juvenile literature.   3. Punic War, 2nd,
218–201 B.C.—Juvenile literature. [1. Hannibal, 247–182 B.C.   2. Generals.
3. Punic War, 2nd, 218–201 B.C.]   I. Title.   II. Series.
DG249.G695   1996
937'.04—dc20   96-7276 CIP AC

CONTENTS

This is the man for whom Africa
Was too small a continent, though it stretched
  from the surf-beaten
Ocean shores of Morocco east to the steamy Nile.
—JUVENAL, ROMAN POET

1

ROME AND CARTHAGE

In 219 B.C. a small group of Roman ambassadors sailed from Rome to the North African city of Carthage. At a meeting with the Carthaginian Senate, the leader of the Romans pointed to his flowing robes in a stately manner and declared that within lay both peace and war. The Carthaginians could choose one or the other. But if Carthage desired peace, the Roman said, they had to surrender Hannibal.

Hannibal was the most powerful Carthaginian general. He was the son of the distinguished Hamilcar Barca, who had created the Carthaginian empire in Spain. Hannibal had just conquered the port city of Saguntum in eastern Spain. The riches of Saguntum were flowing into Carthage, to the delight of the

Carthaginians. Saguntum was an ally of Rome, and Hannibal's capture of it brought the Roman ambassadors to Carthage. The Carthaginians refused to give up Hannibal. To this, the Roman ambassador said, "Then I leave war." And the senators of Carthage replied, "War we take!"

The war declared in 218 B.C. between Rome and Carthage, known as the Second Punic War, lasted until 201 B.C. It threw the Mediterranean world into disorder for nearly two decades. The Carthaginians had refused to surrender Hannibal, and the Second Punic War became his war. Holding his army together through sheer force of character and personal greatness, he marched to the gates of Rome. He shook the foundation of the Roman state and nearly caused it to topple entirely. So great was Hannibal's threat that, even after his defeat, to speak his name struck fear into Roman hearts.

Hannibal's war was not the first between Rome and Carthage, nor was it the last, but it was the most devastating and most decisive. It put Rome in a posi-

The Roman ambassador Quintus Fabius Maximus declares war in the Carthaginian Senate after the Carthaginians refuse to surrender Hannibal.

tion to establish an empire that would last until the Middle Ages. It also plunged Carthage into despair, ending hundreds of years of prosperity.

THE CARTHAGINIAN EMPIRE

According to tradition, the city of Carthage was founded by people from Phoenicia (modern Lebanon) in 814 B.C. It was founded on a small peninsula near the modern city of Tunis, in Tunisia. There were many such Phoenician colonies in North Africa. As the Phoenician sailors forged trade routes around the Mediterranean, settlements sprang up along the North African coast as far as the Pillars of Hercules. There the Mediterranean Sea empties through the Strait of Gibraltar into the Atlantic Ocean.

Carthage soon outdid the other Phoenician settlements and became the busiest trading port in North Africa. The Carthaginians had competed with the Greeks for control of trade routes in the Mediterranean. But after the death of Alexander the Great in 323 B.C., Greece steadily declined as a major power. Carthage leaped into the void, becoming a trade link between east and west, between Europe and Asia. For a time, the Carthaginians were masters of the western Mediterranean and Carthage was the richest city in the world.

When Rome began to grow, Carthage saw it as a

According to legend, Dido fled from the Phoenician city of Tyre after the murder of her husband. She arrived in North Africa and convinced the Libyans to sell her as much land as an oxhide would cover. She then cut the hide into thin strips and laid them around the hill of Byras. This hill later became the citadel of Carthage.

potential challenger. At first, the Romans were a land power. They were satisfied with strengthening their hold on the Italian peninsula. Carthage, on the other hand, was a sea power, with a small population and little need for more land. The two seemed safely out of each other's way. Then, on the island of Sicily, the interests of the two powers clashed.

Sicily lies in the Mediterranean, between the Italian peninsula and Africa. The Carthaginians already held the western corner of the island. When they tried to expand their control of the island in 264 B.C., Rome declared war on them. That conflict, called the First Punic War, took place mostly at sea, where at first the Carthaginians had the advantage. The Romans, however, learned how to build faster and sturdier ships from the Carthaginian vessels that they captured. Their sea forces became stronger, and by 241 B.C. they won major battles at sea. Hamilcar Barca, the father of Hannibal, had been defeating the Romans in Sicily, but he could no longer get supplies after Carthage lost control of the sea.

As a result of the First Punic War, Rome became a major Mediterranean sea power. The Carthaginians, on the other hand, suffered not only defeat at the hands of the Romans but also a revolt of their own soldiers. These men were not really Carthaginians but mercenaries (paid soldiers) from other countries, for Carthage did not have a large enough population

*The city of Messina in Sicily was strategically
important because it is very close to Italy. This
photograph of the city shows the Italian
mainland in the background.*

Hamilcar Barca, Hannibal's father, despised the Romans. After conquering Spain he planned to invade Italy, but he died before he could carry out his plan. Hannibal later marched on Italy to avenge the defeat that the Carthaginians had suffered in the First Punic War.

to fill the ranks of an effective army. The revolt by the mercenaries was crushed after three years of hard fighting by Hamilcar Barca. In the meantime, the Romans took advantage of the Carthaginians' troubles and seized the islands of Sardinia and Corsica from them.

YOUNG SOLDIER HANNIBAL

When peace finally returned to Carthage, Hamilcar Barca began to plan for the future. He realized that Sicily and the other islands of the Mediterranean were lost. But the Carthaginians had connections in Spain, and Hamilcar was determined to carve an empire from the rich lands of that country. One story says that before leaving for Spain in 237 B.C., Hamilcar took his nine-year-old son, Hannibal, to the altar of a Carthaginian god and made him swear that he would always be an enemy of the Roman people. Hannibal then went with Hamilcar to Spain.

The center of Carthaginian power in Spain was the city of New Carthage (modern Cartagena). Hamilcar spent much of his life on campaigns, subduing the Spanish tribes. Hannibal saw firsthand his father's mastery of war.

When Hamilcar died in battle in 230 B.C., his son-in-law, Hasdrubal "the Handsome," became general and continued Carthage's influence in Spain. The

Carthaginian warriors look on as young Hannibal (in the blue sash) takes an oath of eternal hatred of the Romans.

Romans watched as Carthage slowly came back to life after the First Punic War and its Spanish empire grew. In 226 B.C. Hasdrubal signed a treaty with the Romans. The Romans agreed never to send an army south of the Ebro River in northern Spain, and Hasdrubal promised not to send one north of it.

When Hasdrubal was struck down by an angry Spanish tribesman in 221 B.C., the Carthaginians unanimously elected twenty-six-year-old Hannibal to be commander of the army in Spain. Hannibal continued to conquer Spain south of the Ebro, except for the city of Saguntum, an ally of Rome. When Saguntum stirred up trouble between the Carthaginians and the Romans in 219 B.C., Hannibal sacked the city. This set off the Second Punic War. While Rome's ambassadors demanded his surrender in Carthage, Hannibal set off on a long and dangerous journey, with battle elephants marching at the front of his army. His trek would take him into the heart of Roman territory and to the gates of Rome itself.

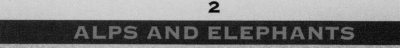

2

ALPS AND ELEPHANTS

Hannibal had learned much in his campaigns against the Spanish tribes. He almost fulfilled his father's ambition of conquering the entire Iberian (Spanish) peninsula. Like Alexander the Great, who named conquered cities after himself, Hannibal left a lasting reminder of his deeds in the names of Spanish places such as Portus Hannibalis, Insula Hannibalis, and Scalae Hannibalis.

Not even his successes in Spain, however, could have prepared Hannibal for the journey that lay ahead. Because Carthage no longer had a great navy, he knew that he had to march his army to Italy by land. Hannibal was familiar with the successes of Alexander the Great in Asia, where Alexander had

Carthaginian merchants sell their wares in a Roman city. The city of Carthage became one of the great trading cities of the ancient world. Carthaginian settlements along the coasts of Africa and Spain were ports for Carthaginian ships doing business around the Mediterranean. The Punic Wars erupted when Rome grew strong enough to challenge Carthage's control of this trade.

defeated his enemies during a long and hazardous land conquest. Hannibal made plans to do the same.

The difference between a heroic undertaking and a foolhardy one often lies only in its success or failure. Hannibal's journey seemed foolhardy and destined to fail. His course would take his army across the Pyrenees mountains into France, across the swift Rhône River, and finally through the rugged Alps. In most of this territory lived hostile tribes.

ON THE MARCH

In the spring of 218 B.C., Hannibal handed over command of the Spanish armies to his brother Hasdrubal and said good-bye to his wife, Imilce, the daughter of a Spanish chieftain. Hannibal probably never saw her again. He then led his troops north toward the Pyrenees and began one of the most famous journeys in history.

Hannibal's army included Libyans and Numidians from North Africa, Iberians and Celtiberians from Spain, and Gauls from Spain, France, and Italy. There

The use of elephants gave Hannibal a great advantage over the Romans in war. This picture shows archers firing from a howdah, or carriage, on an elephant's back.

were ninety thousand foot soldiers, twelve thousand horsemen, and several dozen war elephants. Hannibal used the elephants much as a modern general uses a tank—to break infantry lines and to create fear and disorder. Hannibal's elephants certainly created fear in his enemies, for most of them had never seen such beasts. The elephants also frightened horses, so they were able to disrupt the enemy's cavalry.

In the Pyrenees, Hannibal encountered fierce resistance from local tribes. He lost many of his men in the fighting, and some of the mercenaries turned back, daunted by the prospects of traveling so far. Nevertheless, Hannibal pushed on as quickly as possible. It was essential that he reach the Alps before winter storms made them impassable.

When news of Hannibal's approaching army reached Rome, Italy erupted with activity. The Gauls of northern Italy revolted; they had long been hostile to the Romans. The Romans, who had planned to attack Carthage and New Carthage directly, now had to deal with the rebelling tribes in Italy and the approach of Hannibal. They delayed their attack on Spain. Instead, they sent troops, under the command of Publius Cornelius Scipio, to stop Hannibal at Massilia (modern Marseilles, France).

Massilia lies on the French coast where the Rhône River runs into the Mediterranean Sea. The Rhône is a wide river with a swift current, so it was a

Hannibal's army built enormous rafts to ferry the elephants across the Rhône River.

great obstacle to Hannibal. Scipio's troops set up camp by the sea, assuming that Hannibal would be some time in arriving at Massilia. He did not realize how fast Hannibal was driving his forces.

When news of Hannibal's approach finally reached Scipio, it was too late. Hannibal had moved his entire army across the Rhône, fifty miles (80 km) north of Massilia. The Romans were left holding an empty trap.

Although Hannibal's army had been cut down to fifty thousand infantry, nine thousand horses, and thirty-seven elephants, it was a great feat to ferry this force across the Rhône. To transport the elephants, the men built enormous rafts and covered them with dirt and branches, to give the appearance of solid ground. The elephants were then driven onto the rafts by their handlers, and the rafts were cut free and dragged to the opposite bank. Some elephants panicked and fell off, but they managed to hold up their trunks and swim to shore. Not a single elephant was lost.

INTO THE MOUNTAINS

Hannibal hurried forward in order to outstrip the Romans. Soon the dizzying, snowy peaks of the Alps came into view. Hannibal allowed his weary army a few days' rest, for they surely had doubts about the

No one knows exactly what route Hannibal took across the Alps. Some people think he used one of these passages through the beautiful Chamonix Valley in France.

path ahead. He addressed them (through inter-
preters, since they spoke many languages) with
words of encouragement, reminding them how many
obstacles they had successfully crossed in the past
months. Then they began to wind their way up the
mountain trails.

Never before had elephants crossed the Alps. The
sight of these lumbering beasts, high above the tree
line in the snow, was surely one of the strangest in history. The army did not reach the Alps until late
autumn, and many troops and horses were killed.
Some troops who came from warmer climates died
from the cold. Rations were short, so some died of
hunger. Others died in battles with mountain tribes.
These Celtic people attacked the animals and rolled
big stones downhill. The stones caused men and animals to panic or fall from the narrow mountain passes.

When Hannibal emerged on the Italian side of the

*Hannibal looks back at the
Carthaginian army as it threads
through an alpine pass. Hostile tribes
slowed Hannibal's army by hurling
stones and rolling boulders down at the
army. The icy paths also caused the
elephants to lose their footing.*

Alps, he had lost nearly half of his soldiers and a third of his horses, but there is no record that any of the elephants, surely the most ill-suited to the cold, were lost. The horses were thin and the soldiers, with their long, bearded faces, were nearly starving, yet the men looked down on the fertile plains of Italy, beyond which lay Rome. The news ran throughout Italy: Hannibal has crossed the Alps!

3

CANNAE

Hannibal had completed an epic journey, and with the Alps at his back he set out to confront the Romans. He could not hope for the surrender of Rome unless he defeated the Roman army. Through a series of victories, culminating at Cannae in 216 B.C., Hannibal would nearly succeed.

The Roman army was extremely well equipped and well disciplined. The Romans were also prepared to die defending their homeland. Scipio's troops had gone on to Spain. When he got back to Italy from Massilia, he took command of the Roman forces that had been sent north and set out to meet Hannibal.

Hannibal was eager to face the Roman forces, because he needed to know how many there were

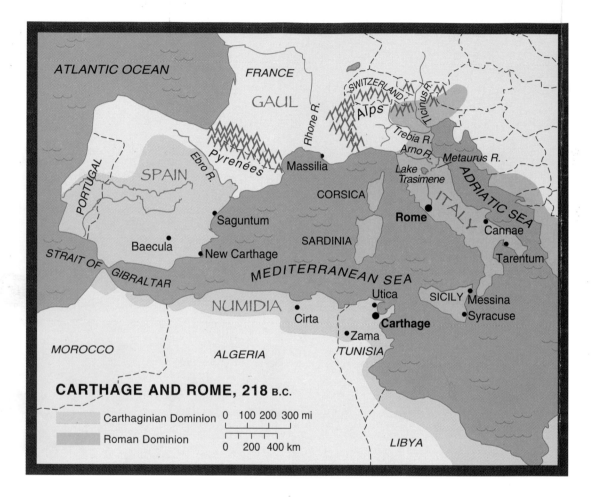

ATLANTIC OCEAN

FRANCE

GAUL

SWITZERLAND

Rhone R.

Ticinus R.

Alps

Trebia R.

Arno R.

Metaurus R.

Pyrenées

Massilia

Lake
Trasimene

ADRIATIC SEA

SPAIN

Ebro R.

CORSICA

ITALY

PORTUGAL

Saguntum

Rome

Cannae

SARDINIA

Baecula

New Carthage

Tarentum

STRAIT OF
GIBRALTAR

MEDITERRANEAN SEA

NUMIDIA

Utica

SICILY

Messina

Cirta

Carthage

Syracuse

MOROCCO

Zama

TUNISIA

ALGERIA

CARTHAGE AND ROME, 218 B.C.

Carthaginian Dominion

Roman Dominion

0   100 200 300 mi

0   200 400 km

LIBYA

and what sort of man was in command. For Hannibal, war was a personal matter. He benefited from knowledge of the character of his enemy. When he could, Hannibal exploited the weaknesses not only of an opposing army but also of its commander.

EARLY BATTLES

The first skirmish between the two forces occurred when Hannibal's Numidian horsemen, a swift and lightly-armed cavalry, met the advancing Romans at the Ticinus River. The Romans retreated, but not before Scipio was wounded. One story says that Scipio's son, Scipio Africanus, saved him by charging into the battle and carrying him to safety. Scipio Africanus was learning a great deal from watching Hannibal beat the Romans.

Soon Scipio was retreating to the south with Hannibal in pursuit. The Roman general Tiberius Sempronius Longus arrived with reinforcements from Sicily. This would appear to have tipped the scales in favor of the Romans, but Longus and Scipio disagreed about how to deal with Hannibal. Longus was eager for a battle, and in December of 218 B.C. Hannibal sent out his Numidian cavalry to lure Longus into a trap at the Trebia River.

Longus fell for the trap, pursuing the Numidian cavalry with not only his horsemen but with Roman

Scipio Africanus rescues his fallen father by charging into the thick of the battle and carrying him to safety.

legions as well. When the Numidians, with the Romans in hot pursuit, reached Hannibal's main force, they veered off to the sides of the battlefield. The Romans were left staring dumbly at Hannibal's infantry, headed by charging elephants. The Numidian horsemen swung around to attack the Romans from the rear. When Carthaginian forces, which Hannibal had hidden before the battle, emerged behind the Romans, the trap was fully sprung. The Carthaginians had encircled the Roman army and proceeded to destroy nearly three-quarters of the Roman force.

It was a terrible defeat for Rome, where panic broke out in the streets. Winter weather, however, stopped the Carthaginian advance. Many of Hannibal's men and animals died in the cold. By spring, only one elephant was left alive. Meanwhile, the Romans sent new legions north to meet Hannibal. The Romans watched every road to see which route Hannibal would take toward Rome. In the early spring of 217 B.C. Hannibal set out by an unexpected route, through the swampy lands of the lower Arno River valley.

LAKE TRASIMENE

The swamp took a further toll on Hannibal's army. Many of the remaining baggage animals died. The swamp offered few places for shelter or sleep, and many soldiers became ill. Hannibal himself, riding the last elephant, lost sight in one eye from an infection. Nevertheless, by traveling through the swamp, Hannibal had slipped his army past the watchful guard of the Romans.

Hannibal expected the Romans to attack him as soon as they heard where he was, so he set another trap. Lake Trasimene provided a natural bottleneck, with hills on both sides of the water. Hannibal placed part of his troops inside a narrow pass as bait, and the Romans, commanded by the consul Flaminius, advanced eagerly into the U-shaped jaws of this trap. As soon as the Romans pounced, the jaws of the trap clamped shut.

A heavy mist covered the entire area that day, and the Carthaginians emerged swiftly from the fog to cut down the Romans. The slaughter continued for three hours. Fifteen thousand Romans were killed, including Flaminius. Hannibal took another fifteen thousand Romans prisoner.

The Romans expected Hannibal to march directly on Rome. They elected Quintus Fabius Maximus

Roman women throw up their arms and beg the gods to save their city from Hannibal.

dictator and Marcus Minucius Rufus as his assistant. As dictator, Fabius was given the responsibilities of preparing the defenses of the city and regrouping the Roman army. Fabius carried out his duties with calm determination. This set a good example for the people of Rome, and the panic began to quiet.

Hannibal did not march on Rome, for he lacked the manpower and equipment to lay siege. Instead the troops moved to the Adriatic coast where they could rest and heal their wounds. Fabius kept the Roman army in contact with Hannibal, while Hannibal confined himself to ravaging the land for food and supplies. Fabius followed a policy of patient delay. He did not wish to fight poorly and give Hannibal another victory.

By the summer of 217 B.C., the Roman people had become tired of Fabius's inactivity. Minucius, who was confident and ambitious, was elected co-dictator, something that had never been done before. He set out to meet Hannibal. Hannibal exploited the eagerness of Minucius, as he had that of Longus and Flaminius. He attacked, but forces led by Fabius managed to save Minucius. Fabius continued his policy of delay until late in 217, when his six-month dictatorship ended.

Fabius effectively wore down the Carthaginian forces. They could not receive reinforcements or replacements for those who fell in battle. But Fabius

In Campania in 217 B.C. Hannibal lashed bundles of sticks onto the horns of oxen and set them afire. The oxen, led by Carthaginian scouts, appeared in the dark of night to be an army on the move. This decoy drew the attention of the Romans while Hannibal slipped away to his winter camp at Apulia. Because of such unusual strategies, the Romans called Hannibal "the wizard."

could not convince the Romans that an enemy army—one that had severely beaten Rome twice already—should be allowed to feed off the rich lands around them unharassed. Rome again prepared for battle: the Carthaginians must be destroyed.

MEETING AT CANNAE

Many Romans believed that if they could just field a large enough army, they could defeat Hannibal. In June 216 B.C. a Roman army under the command of the consuls Aemilius Paulus and Terentius Varro marched out to meet Hannibal near Cannae, a village Hannibal had seized for its grain supply.

At Cannae Hannibal did not have an advantage provided by the land like the trap around Lake Trasimene. Even without it, though, he set up the same kind of trap using only his troops. The center of Hannibal's infantry, the Gauls and Spaniards, withdrew when they met the Roman infantry, while his African infantry on the sides remained stationary. By this strategy, Hannibal led the main part of the Roman army into a U-shaped trap (as if into a sack), with Carthaginians on three sides. He then pulled the strings to tie the sack's open end: his Numidian light cavalry and Carthaginian heavy cavalry swung around with frightening speed and cut off the Romans' only retreat.

At Cannae Hannibal defeated a Roman army larger than his own by drawing the Roman center forward and then advancing the wings of his army to envelop the Romans. This is considered one of the classic maneuvers in the history of warfare.

The slaughter that followed was the worst in Roman history. The inexperienced Roman soldiers panicked. Well over half of the Roman soldiers died in a day. Paulus and many other important Romans were slain. Hannibal had defeated not only the largest Roman army ever assembled, but also the theory that a smaller army could be overrun simply by larger numbers. Young Scipio Africanus, who survived Cannae, learned the lesson well. Scipio realized that Hannibal would only be defeated by Hannibal's methods.

The Battle of Cannae was the final blow of a furious attack on Rome, coming after the moral victory of crossing the Alps and the military victories at Ticinus, Trebia, and Trasimene. At Cannae the Roman army was dealt the greatest defeat it had ever suffered. Hannibal had thus avenged the Carthaginian defeat in the First Punic War. He had hacked at the Roman state until nothing remained but its roots. These roots were law and order, established by the republican government.

The Battle of Cannae caused the Roman state to teeter, but it did not fall. From its roots the Roman state would grow back. The survival of Rome after the disaster at Cannae prompted the Roman historian Livy to write, "No other nation could have suffered such a tremendous disaster and not been destroyed."

4

AT THE GATES OF ROME

Each day after Cannae, the Romans expected Hannibal to march on Rome. But he did not attack. Even his own troops did not understand why Hannibal did not march directly on Rome. The master of his cavalry, Marhabal, expressed the general frustration when he said, "You know how to win a victory, but not how to use one!"

Hannibal knew his weakness: he had neither the troops nor the equipment to attack Rome. It was a frustrating victory. Hannibal had defeated the army that stood between him and Rome, but the city could not be taken. So Hannibal would linger in Italy until 203 B.C., coming no closer to defeating Rome. Time, in fact, proved only to weaken his position.

SCIPIO IN SPAIN

Hannibal kept in touch with Carthage from the east (Adriatic) coast of Italy. Carthage prepared to send reinforcements. Most of these troops, however, never reached Hannibal. Instead they were sent to Spain, where Rome had been successfully attacking the Carthaginian forces. While the policy of Fabius—the policy of delay—was once again adopted by Rome after the defeat at Cannae, an active war was waged in Spain.

In 210 B.C. Scipio Africanus was elected to command the Roman forces in Spain. He had

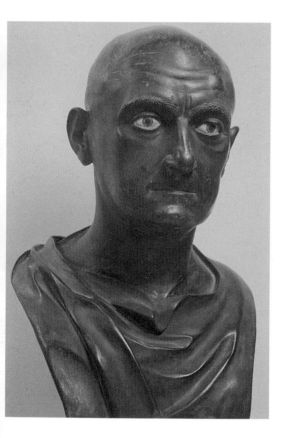

Scipio Africanus used many of Hannibal's own strategies to defeat the Carthaginians. He sacked Cartagena, the center of Carthaginian power in Spain, and eventually brought the war to Hannibal's homeland, guessing correctly that Hannibal would go back to defend Carthage.

witnessed Hannibal's tactics in northern Italy and then at Cannae. He decided to put his knowledge of war to the test in Spain. By 209 B.C. Scipio had sacked New Carthage (Cartagena), the center of Carthaginian power in Spain.

Scipio's victory in Spain provided the Romans with a boost in morale. They also took gold, silver, and other riches from New Carthage. Rome had lost almost all its wealth because of the war with Hannibal, and it needed to refill its treasury.

Rome was once again growing strong. The riches of Scipio's victories helped to pay for new troops and the construction of new ships. Rome conquered all of Sicily, which was still important for controlling trade routes in the Mediterranean. Because of this, the Carthaginians would not be able to resupply Hannibal by sea. While Rome's fortunes rose, Hannibal's fell.

Hannibal had entered into an alliance with King Philip V of Macedon (part of modern Greece) hoping to quickly receive supplies and troops. But war came to Greece before Philip could send Hannibal support, and the two allies became useless to each other. Hannibal's brother Hasdrubal marched toward Italy from Spain. The only possibility of victory for the Carthaginians was for the two brothers to capture Rome together. Hasdrubal crossed all the obstacles that Hannibal had crossed and successfully entered Italy in 207 B.C. Once again elephants lumbered through the perilous Alpine passages. Hannibal moved north to meet up with him.

THE DEATH OF HASDRUBAL

To arrange a meeting place, Hasdrubal sent messengers on horseback to search for Hannibal. The written message fell into the hands of the Roman general Claudius Nero. Nero now knew what Hannibal did not—the exact location of Hasdrubal. Nero's army was still in contact with Hannibal's, but he slipped most of his troops out from their position without Hannibal noticing and made a wild dash north. Nero's troops reinforced those of the generals Livius and Porcius near Hasdrubal's army.

Nero tried to hide his soldiers in the tents of Livius's army, but Hasdrubal suspected what was happening. Thrown into wild despair by the thought that his brother may have been defeated in the south,

Hannibal is startled when the Romans toss the severed head of his brother Hasdrubal into the Carthaginian camp. When he saw that his brother had been defeated, Hannibal said, "I see there the fate of Carthage."

he retreated to the Metaurus River. The Romans pursued him.

Hasdrubal's army was thrown into confusion. Some of the allied tribes deserted, and the Gauls became unruly. When the Romans attacked, even Hasdrubal's war elephants panicked and were driven wildly into the ranks of the Carthaginian soldiers. Hasdrubal, seeing that all was lost, drew his sword and charged the Roman line. He died, and with him went the last chance for a Carthaginian victory over Rome.

After his victory, Nero quickly withdrew to the south to keep Hannibal in check. Nero conveyed the news of his victory to Hannibal by tossing Hasdrubal's severed head into the Carthaginian camp in the dark of night. Hannibal looked upon the head of his brother and said, "I see there the fate of Carthage."

When the news of Hasdrubal's defeat reached Rome, the city erupted in celebration, and Nero and Livius, the consuls, were received as heroes. Roman pride was returning. Soon Scipio, in Spain, gave the Romans more to celebrate. In 206 B.C. he defeated Hannibal's younger brother, Mago, and General Hasdrubal Gisco (no relation to Hannibal) at Baecula. This final defeat of the Carthaginians in Spain insured that Hannibal would never again receive reinforcements by land. It also gave Scipio the chance to return to Italy.

SCIPIO IN NORTH AFRICA

Scipio proposed an invasion of North Africa, but other Roman leaders bitterly opposed the idea. They pointed out that Hannibal was still in Italy, and Scipio should concentrate on the closest, and most threatening, enemy. But the farsighted Scipio had already mapped his strategy. The Roman Senate finally gave Scipio the right to take the war to Carthage. They added the condition that all responsibility for failure would be his own.

After training his army in Sicily—where he recruited soldiers who had been defeated at Cannae—Scipio left for North Africa in the spring of 204 B.C. The people of Carthage were very shaken by the arrival of Scipio, but they did not send for Hannibal right away. Hasdrubal Gisco, by that time the commander of the Carthaginian forces in North Africa, prepared to field an army.

The Numidian tribes, from which Hannibal had recruited his horsemen, came to play a larger part in the struggle between Rome and Carthage. The strongest leader in Numidia (modern Algeria) was Syphax. Syphax had already entered into and broken alliances with the Romans. He then confirmed his allegiance to Carthage by marrying Sophonisba, the beautiful daughter of Hasdrubal Gisco.

This alliance drove Syphax's rival, Massinissa, to

join the Romans, for Massinissa and Syphax were bitter enemies and both had wanted to marry Sophonisba. Whichever side Syphax chose, Massinissa would choose the opposite. Massinissa's Numidian troops joined Scipio, who was attacking the town of Utica to the west of Carthage. Syphax joined the forces of Hasdrubal Gisco.

Scipio entered into peace negotiations with the Carthaginians and Syphax. But this was only a trick: Scipio did not have the intention or the right to make

peace with Carthage. He did it in order to learn more about the enemy camp. The peace negotiations caused the Carthaginians to drop their guard, and Scipio struck.

One night in the early spring of 203 B.C., Scipio secretly moved his troops to the edge of the Carthaginian camps, while Massinissa's horsemen rode among the enemy and set fire to their huts. As the wind carried the fire from hut to hut, the Carthaginians and Syphax's soldiers emerged only to be cut down by the waiting Romans. Both camps were left in ruins, and most of Hasdrubal Gisco's forces died.

Scipio Africanus, center, speaks with the Numidian king Syphax, whom he has taken prisoner. Syphax's wife, Sophonisba, looks on from the left while a servant offers her a drink from a golden cup. Sophonisba had charmed both Massinissa and Syphax, making their rivalry more intense.

The two armies clashed a second time. The Romans destroyed Hasdrubal Gisco's army and slaughtered many Numidians. Massinissa pursued Syphax to Cirta, the capital of Numidia, where he captured Syphax and made himself king of Numidia. He also took Sophonisba for himself. Scipio later reminded the hot-headed Massinissa that Sophonisba was a Roman prisoner and would be paraded in chains through Rome. Rather than submit to this humiliation, Sophonisba killed herself by drinking a cup of poison.

The defeat of Hasdrubal Gisco and Syphax left Carthage undefended. The city now experienced the same fear that had gripped Rome since Hannibal's arrival in Italy. They had only one hope—Hannibal was called back to defend Carthage.

After his victory over Syphax, Massinissa took Sophonisba for his own. This displeased Scipio Africanus, who wanted to parade her in triumph in Rome. Sophonisba did not want to submit to either position, so she poisoned herself, as portrayed here.

5

ZAMA AND AFTER

With his victory in Africa, Scipio proved to be a master of strategy and a worthy opponent of Hannibal. He had done what all the Roman generals could not: force Hannibal from Italy. Carthaginian ships successfully removed Hannibal from the Italian peninsula and carried him back to Carthage. That in itself was a difficult task, because the Romans controlled the sea.

Rome had slipped from Hannibal's grasp just as Spain had slipped from the grasp of Carthage. Carthage was now fighting for its life. The armies of Hannibal and Scipio met near the town of Zama in 202 B.C. When they encamped across from one another,

*Hannibal (center) and Scipio (right) meet
face to face for the first time at Zama.*

Hannibal and Scipio rode out to meet each other on the battlefield. Hannibal, now a one-eyed, grizzled battle veteran, offered to surrender. He probably did not expect Scipio to accept, and he was right. The meeting was more for the men to satisfy their curiosity. Two great generals—Hannibal, the teacher, and Scipio, the pupil—met face to face.

The pupil had learned well. Most of all, he had learned the usefulness of Hannibal's Numidian cavalry. With Massinissa's tribesmen, Scipio's horsemen outnumbered Hannibal's. Hannibal relied instead on his elephants to break the Roman troop lines.

On the day of the battle, Hannibal placed eighty elephants in front of his foot soldiers to lead the charge. The elephants were newly trained, and the Romans turned many of them back with great trumpet blasts and shouts. Some of the elephants turned and crashed into Hannibal's lines, causing much destruction.

When Hannibal's foot soldiers clashed with the Romans, both sides held their ground. Meanwhile, Massinissa's Numidians had beaten Hannibal's cavalry and chased them for some time. When Massinissa returned to the battle, the outcome was decided. His horsemen attacked the Carthaginians from the sides and the rear, while the Romans pushed Hannibal's army into their grasp. Hannibal had been beaten by the same strategy he had used at Cannae. He suffered

At the Battle of Zama, Hannibal's army included many weary veterans and inexperienced recruits. Even some of the elephants were not properly trained. The Romans confused the charging elephants with trumpet blasts.

his first and last major defeat. With it came the end of Carthaginian influence around the Mediterranean and the end of the Second Punic War.

LIFE IN EXILE

Hannibal had waged war in Italy for sixteen years. He had ravaged the countryside, destroyed or frustrated great Roman armies, and shaken the Roman Republic. The Battle of Zama signaled the end of his great military career, but not the end of Carthage. Hannibal urged the Carthaginians to beg for peace, which the Romans granted in 201 B.C.

Hannibal helped to reform the corrupt government of Carthage while remaining in charge of a small army, which was allowed under the peace treaty with Rome. Although his reforms helped to increase the stability and prosperity of Carthage, they angered the powerful aristocrats who controlled the government. The Romans were already nervous about Carthage's quick economic recovery. Then the Carthaginian aristocrats told them Hannibal was plotting another war. In 195 B.C. the Romans demanded his arrest. Hannibal fled to the court of King Antiochus the Great in Syria, beginning a life of wandering and exile.

Hannibal eventually settled in the Black Sea kingdom of Bithynia, where King Prusias I was at war with an ally of Rome. Hannibal assisted Prusias in this war. The Romans heard of Hannibal's new activities, and in 183 B.C. they demanded that Prusias hand him over as the price of keeping peace with Rome.

Roman troops moved on Hannibal's house in

As the Romans close in on Hannibal, he raises his fist in a final gesture of defiance before drinking a cup of poison. By killing himself he escapes the clutch of the Romans one last time.

Bithynia, hoping to capture the great warlord by surprise. When they burst into his house, Hannibal lay dead, having just drunk a cup of poison. By his own suicide, Hannibal had vanished one last time before the advance of his Roman enemies.

Carthage faced the wrath of Rome in the coming years. In 149 B.C. Rome invaded Carthage, and the Third Punic War erupted. There was no Hannibal in that war, and the Romans completely destroyed Carthage. A century later, Julius Caesar built a Roman colony on its ruins.

The legacy of Hannibal's war on Italy was the expansion of Roman power. Rome had survived its greatest threat, and Hannibal's threat had hurled Rome into the center of Mediterranean events. After the death of Hannibal and the destruction of Carthage, Rome's power grew until all of the Mediterranean and most of Europe fell under its sway. But the Romans never forgot Hannibal. And even after his death, the saying, "Hannibal is at the gates," would frighten the children of Rome.

TIMELINE

264–241 B.C.	Hamilcar Barca, Hannibal's father, leads Carthaginians in First Punic War
247 B.C.	Hannibal born in Carthage
238 B.C.	Hamilcar makes Hannibal swear to be eternal enemy of Rome
230 B.C.	Hamilcar dies in battle; Hasdrubal "the Handsome" takes command of Carthaginian forces
221 B.C.	Hasdrubal killed; Hannibal made commander of forces
219 B.C.	Hannibal sacks city of Saguntum; Second Punic War begins
218 B.C.	Hannibal leads army over Pyrenees, across Rhône River, and over Alps into Italy
late 218 B.C.	Hannibal defeats armies of Scipio and Longus at Trebia River
217 B.C.	Battle at Lake Trasimene; Hannibal decimates Roman army under Flaminius
216 B.C.	Battle of Cannae; Hannibal annihilates Roman forces
209 B.C.	Scipio sacks New Carthage (Cartagena) in Spain
207 B.C.	Hasdrubal marches with army from Spain to Italy to bolster Hannibal's forces; Nero's army defeats Hasdrubal's forces and kills Hasdrubal
204 B.C.	Scipio lands in Africa, receives support of Massinissa
202 B.C.	Battle of Zama; Scipio and Massinissa defeat Hannibal, bringing Second Punic War to an end
201 B.C.	Rome agrees to peace treaty with Carthaginians; Hannibal retains small army
200 B.C.	Hannibal becomes chief magistrate of Carthage, remains in power for five years
195 B.C.	Romans suspect Hannibal of new plot; Hannibal flees to court of King Antiochus in Syria
192–183 B.C.	Hannibal assists Antiochus and later King Prusias I of Bithynia in ineffectual wars against Rome
183 or 182 B.C.	Hannibal commits suicide in Bithynia to avoid capture by Romans
149–146 B.C.	Third Punic War; Romans destroy Carthage

FOR MORE INFORMATION

FOR FURTHER READING

Hirsh, Marilyn. *Hannibal and His 37 Elephants*. New York: Holiday House, 1977.

Jacobs, William J. *Hannibal: An African Hero*. New York: McGraw-Hill, 1973.

Weble, Robert. N. *Hannibal: Invader from Carthage*. New York: Franklin Watts, 1968.

FOR ADVANCED READERS

Bradford, Ernle. *Hannibal*. New York: Dorset Press, 1981.

Hart, B. H. Liddell. *Scipio Africanus: Greater Than Napoleon*. London: Greenhill Books, 1926.

Livy. *The War With Hannibal*. Translated by Aubrey De Selincourt. New York: Penguin Books, 1965.

Polybius. *The Histories*. Translated by W. R. Patton. Cambridge: Loeb Classical Library, 1922.

INTERNET SITES

Home pages and directories will link you to a myriad of Web sites about the ancient Mediterranean world:

Exploring Ancient World Cultures (University of Evansville):
    http://cedar.evansville.edu/~wcweb/wc101/
ArchNet (University of Connecticut):
    http://spirit.lib.uconn.edu/archaeology.html
ROMARCH, a home page on archaeology in Italy and the Roman
    provinces:
    http://personal-www.umich.edu/~pfoss/ROMARCH.html
The Ancient World Web:
    http://atlantic.evsc.virginia.edu/julia/AncientWorld.html

INDEX

Page numbers in *italics* refer to illustrations

Robert Green is a freelance writer who lives in New York City. He holds a B.A. in English literature from Boston University and is the author of *"Vive la France": The French Resistance during World War II.* He has also written biographies of five other important figures of the ancient world: *Alexander the Great, Cleopatra, Herod the Great, Julius Caesar,* and *Tutankhamun.*